COMMUNITY HEROES

A Guide to Being Brave in the Face of the Coronavirus

Written by Renée Lyons, Ph.D.
Illustrated by Sarah Rose Lyons

SCIENCE
LOCALLY RELEVANT **GLOBALLY IMPACTFUL**

SCIENCE
LIFE SCIENCES OUTREACH CENTER

ABOUT THIS PUBLICATION: This publication was created through a collaboration between the Clemson University Life Sciences Outreach Center, an outreach of Clemson University's College of Science, and Clemson-area artist Sarah Rose Lyons. Find out more about the Clemson University Life Sciences Outreach Center at CLEMSON.EDU/CENTERS-INSTITUTES/CULSOC. Special thanks to the Prisma Health Team for reviewing and providing guidance on this publication. Find out more at PRISMAHEALTH.ORG. All proceeds from the sale of this book will go directly to offsetting the cost of production. Neither Clemson University, the author nor the illustrator will receive any revenues.

ABOUT THE ARTIST: Sarah Rose Lyons is an artist and illustrator who focuses her artwork on creating visual metaphors of the environment. Her art is a catalyst for change that pushes the viewer into creating a better story for themselves and for the world in which they live. Check out Sarah's artwork at SARAHROSELYONS.COM.

PRODUCTION ASSISTANCE: College of Science Communications and Marketing Department. Jim Melvin, director; Pete Martin, online and print media coordinator.

———————

What about you?
What have you heard?
How are you feeling
about it?

SCIENCE
LOCALLY-RELEVANT GLOBALLY IMPACT

Did you know that the
coronavirus is actually a
tiny little germ?

Well, it is!
And sometimes tiny little
germs can make us feel sick.

Have you ever had a cold?
Well, a cold is caused by a
little germ too! Just like a
cold, the coronavirus makes
people sick for a little while.

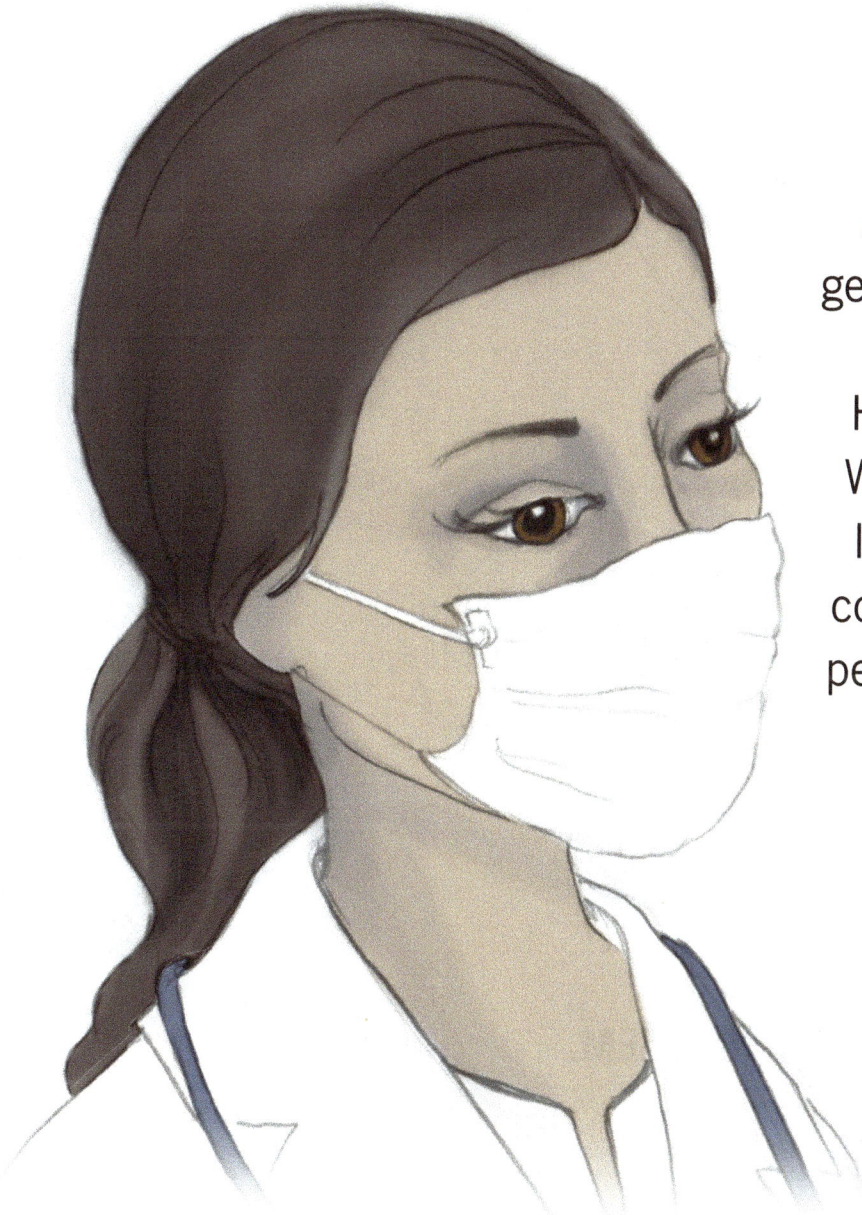

IMMUNE SYSTEM
CAST OF CHARACTERS

ANTIBODIES

CORONAVIRUS

WHITE BLOOD CELLS

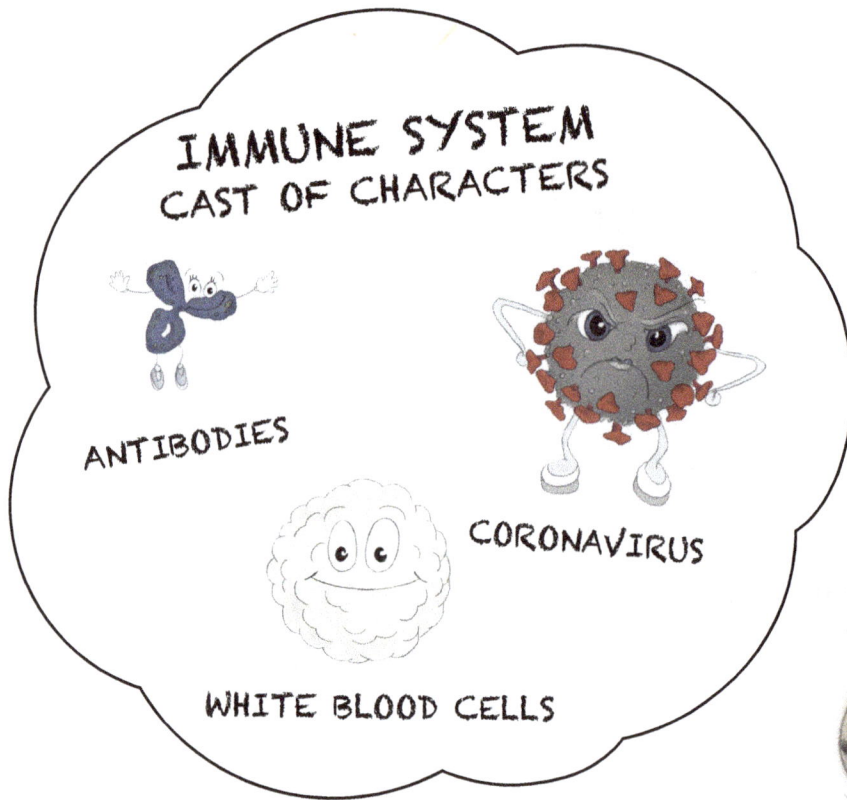

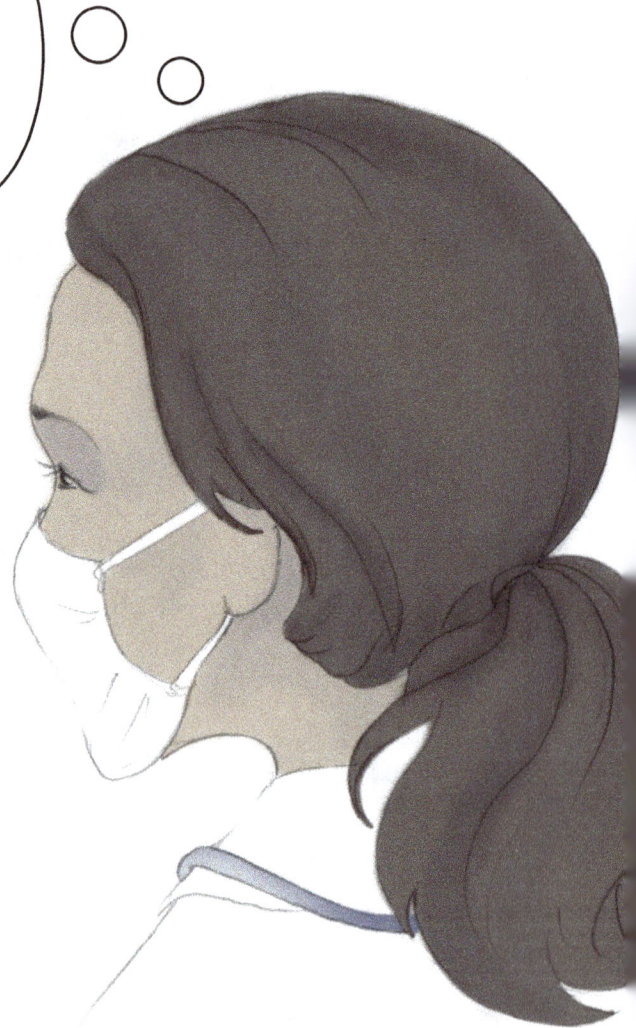

No one wants to feel sick, but the good news is that our bodies have a special army called **THE IMMUNE SYSTEM**.

Our immune system army can fight off little germs like the coronavirus.

Think about the last time you had a cold. How long did you feel sick? You probably felt much better in just a few days!

That was your immune system fighting off the cold germ.

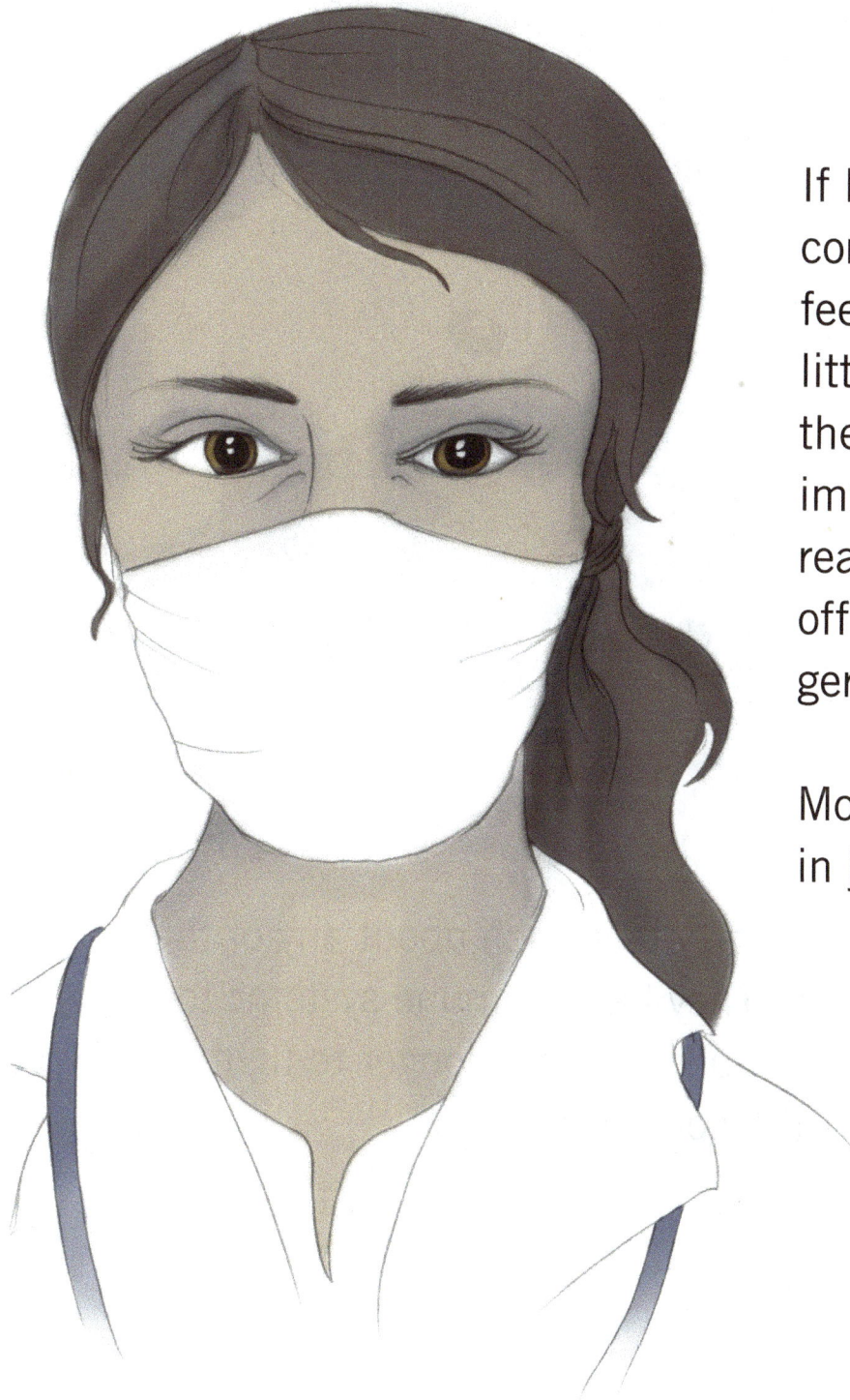

If kids get the coronavirus, they may feel like they just have a little cold. That's because their bodies' special immune system army is really good at fighting off all of the coronavirus germs.

Most kids will feel better in just a few days!

SCIENCE
LOCALLY RELEVANT GLOBALLY IMPACTFUL

I don't want you to worry too much about any of the adults that you love. They have immune systems too! It just may take them a little while longer to fight off the coronavirus.

CLEMSON.EDU/SCIENCE

SCIENCE
LOCALLY RELEVANT GLOBALLY IMPACTFUL

Luckily for all of us, our bodies' special immune system army isn't the only superhero helping fight off the coronavirus. Doctors, nurses and scientists are helping too!

CLEMSON.EDU/SCIENCE

There is a lot you can do to help your community! If all of us work together to help prevent the spread of the coronavirus, we can protect each other from getting sick!
I'm not a doctor or a scientist! How can I help my community?

You can help by **COVERING YOUR MOUTH AND NOSE WITH A TISSUE WHEN YOU COUGH OR SNEEZE**. Be sure to throw your tissue away in the trash can because it may have the coronavirus on it!

You can help by
**WASHING
YOUR HANDS**!

Soap destroys the coronavirus! But only if you wash your hands long enough. To make sure you have destroyed all of the coronavirus germs, sing "Happy Birthday" two times!

Make sure there are plenty of bubbles!

SCIENCE
LOCALLY RELEVANT GLOBALLY IMPACTFUL

Do I need to wash my hands 10,000 times a day?!

No, here are the times you need to wash them:
- ✔ When you come inside after playing or going to the store.
- ✔ Before you eat.
- ✔ After blowing your nose, coughing or sneezing.
- ✔ After using the bathroom.

Masks can be helpful if they are worn the right way. It's especially important for doctors, nurses, people who are sick and people caring for the sick to wear masks!

But masks only help if you keep washing your hands, covering your mouth when you cough or sneeze and staying a safe distance away from people who may be sick.

CLEMSON.EDU/SCIENCE

YOU CAN HELP PROTECT YOUR FRIENDS AND YOUR ENTIRE COMMUNITY BY STAYING AT HOME. This may mean you can't go to school, soccer practice or play with your friends for a while.

The coronavirus spreads from one person to another super fast. If one person is sick, whomever they are playing with or spending time with can also catch the virus. Don't worry, this won't last forever thanks to all of the superheroes fighting against the coronavirus!

It's going to be so much fun when we can all play together again!

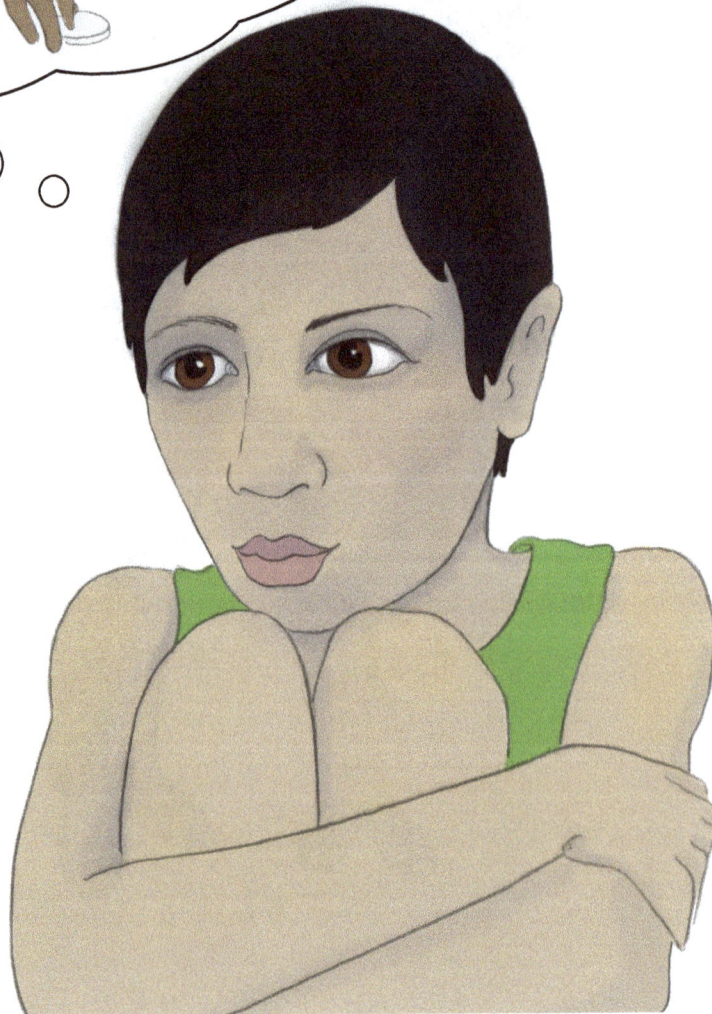

ONLY GO OUT WHEN YOU REALLY NEED TO.

And when you are out, keep a safe distance away from other people who aren't in your family.

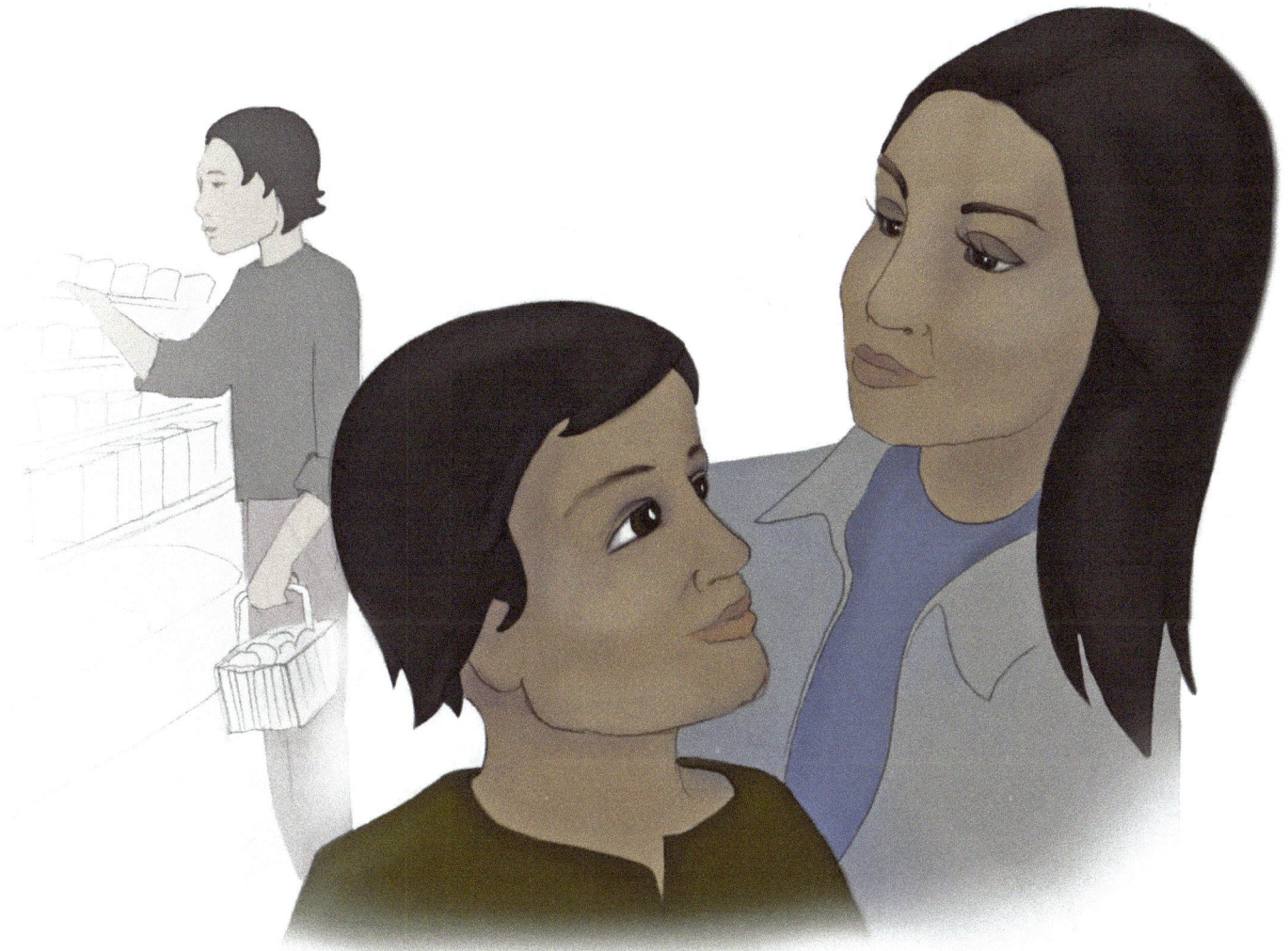

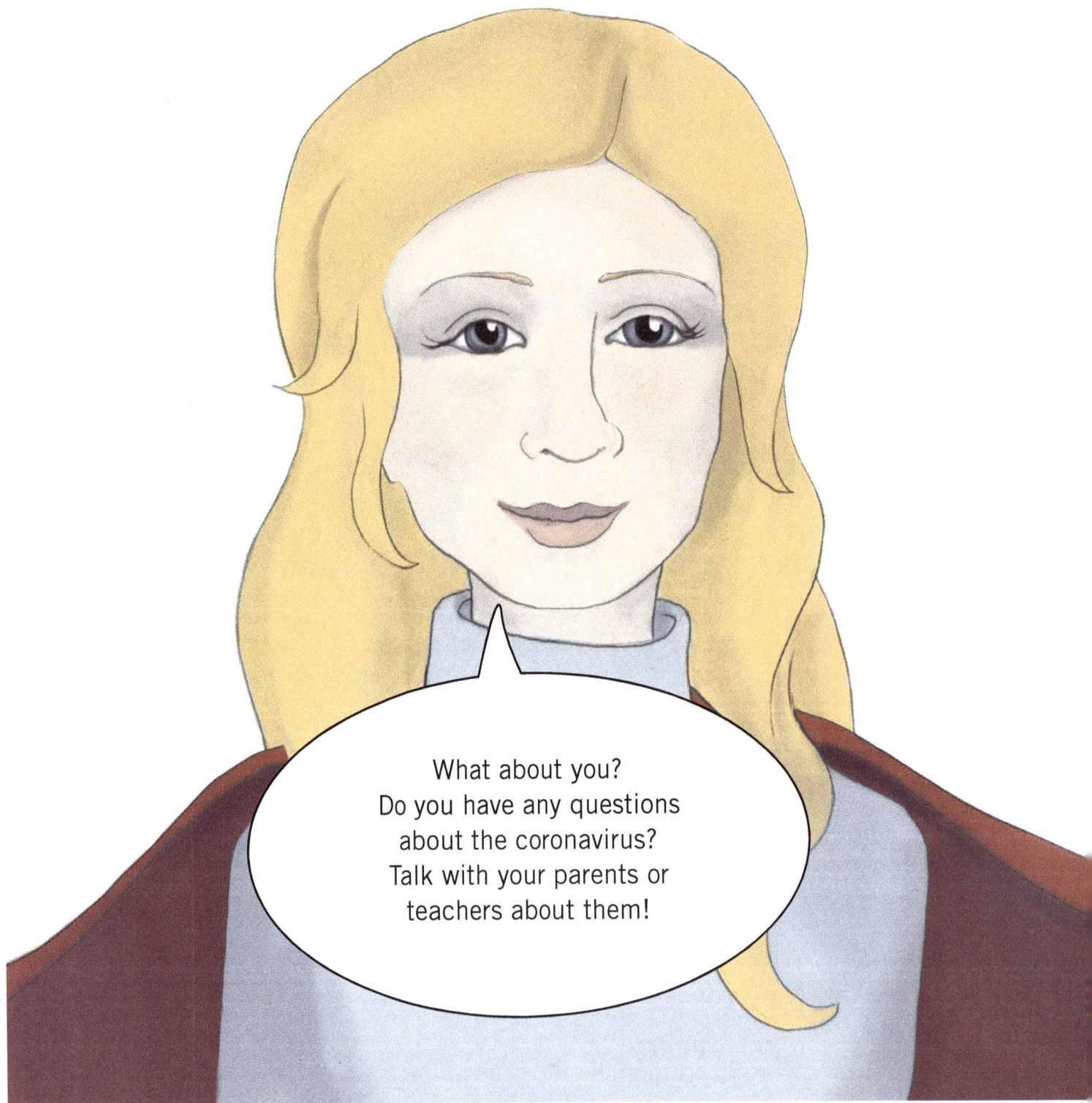

Until next time my fellow superheroes!
Let's keep doing our part to keep everyone in
our community healthy!

www.ingramcontent.com/pod-product-compliance
Lightning Source LLC
Chambersburg PA
CBHW081252040426
42452CB00015B/2800